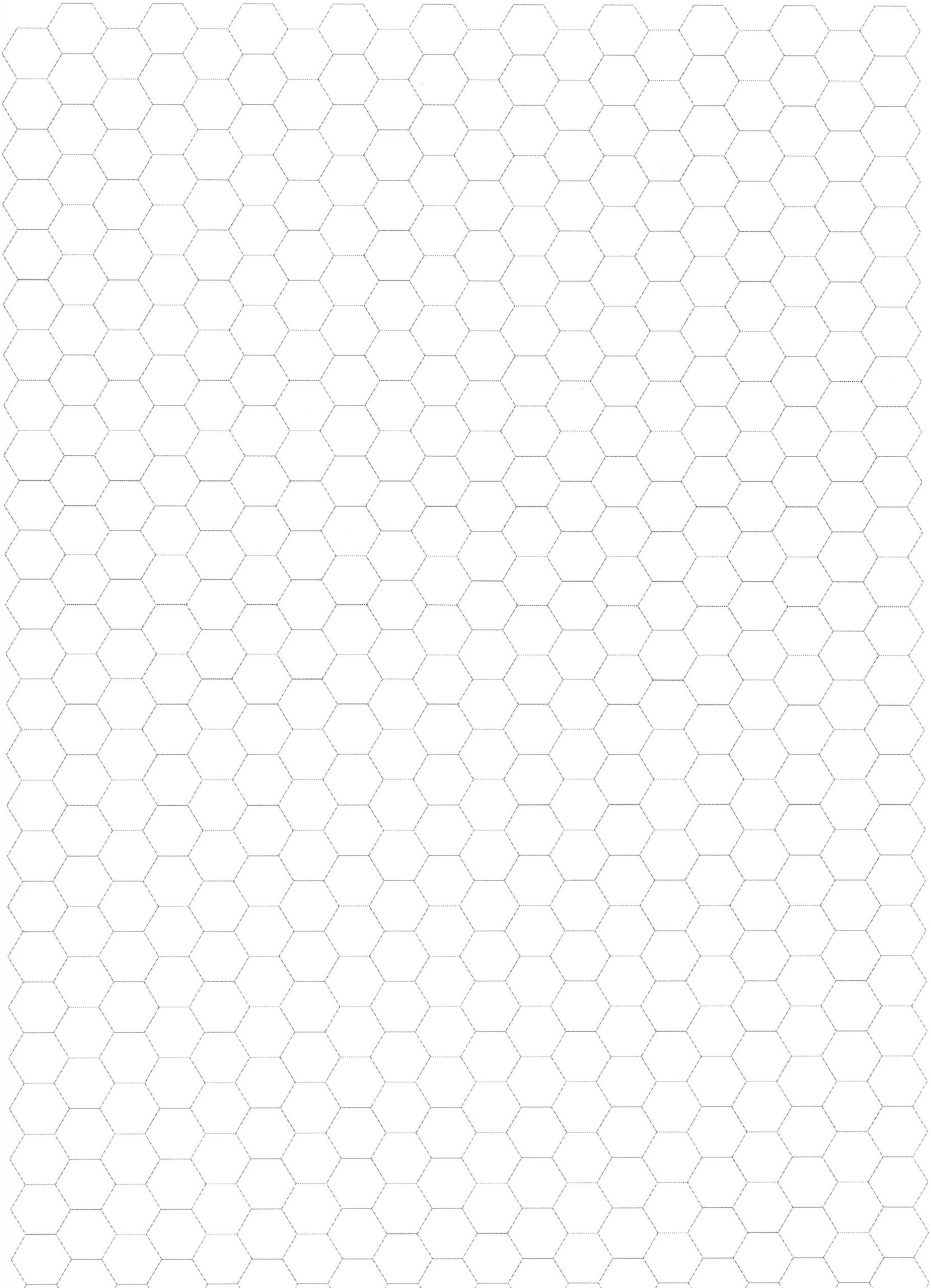

Made in the USA
Columbia, SC
06 December 2019

84400726R00067